SCRIPTURAL
WORSHIP AIDS

SCRIPTURAL WORSHIP AIDS

LeRoy Koopman, Compiler

BAKER BOOK HOUSE
Grand Rapids, Michigan

ISBN: 0-8010-5392-7

Printed in the United States of America

PREFACE

This collection of Scriptural worship aids grew out of my personal needs while leading worship services in the pastorate. I wished to use as many Scriptural sentences as possible, but found both the liturgy and the hymnal to be limited in number and scope. This volume, I believe, will provide for the busy pastor an easy access to a wide variety of Scriptural sentences for virtually every part of the worship service.

CONTENTS

INVOCATIONS

Hear, O Lord, when we* cry aloud,
    be gracious to us and answer us!
Thou hast said, "Seek ye my face."
Our hearts say to thee,
    "Thy face, Lord, do we seek."
    Hide not thy face from us.
Turn not thy servants away in anger,
    thou who has been our help.
Cast us not off, forsake us not,
    O God of our salvation!
Teach us thy way, O Lord;
    and lead us on a level path.

Ps. 27:7-9, 11a

Lord, thou hast been our dwelling place
    in all generations.
Before the mountains were brought forth,
    or ever thou hadst formed the earth and the world,
    from everlasting to everlasting thou art God.
For a thousand years in thy sight
    are but as yesterday when it is past,
    or as a watch in the night.

Ps. 90:1, 2, 4

*Original pronouns are singular.

*We through the abundance of thy steadfast love
   will enter thy house,
We will worship toward thy holy temple
   in the fear of thee.
Lead us, O Lord, in thy righteousness
   because of our enemies;
   make thy way straight before us.

Ps. 5:7, 8

Let the words of our* mouths
   and the meditations of our hearts
      be acceptable in thy sight,
         O Lord, our rock and our redeemer.

Ps. 19:14

As a hart longs
      for flowing streams,
   so longs *our souls
      for thee, O God.
Our souls thirst for God,
   for the living God.

Ps. 42:1, 2

*Original pronouns are singular.

Great and wonderful are thy deeds,
　　O Lord God the Almighty!
Just and true are thy ways,
　　O King of the ages!

Who shall not fear and glorify thy name, O Lord?
For thou alone art holy.
All nations shall come and worship thee,
for thy judgments have been revealed.

Rev. 15:3, 4

*We give thee thanks, O Lord,
　　with the whole heart;
　　　before the gods we sing thy praise;
We bow down toward thy holy temple
　　and give thanks to thy name
　　　for thy steadfast love and thy faithfulness;
　　for thou hast exalted above everything
　　　thy name and thy word.

Ps. 138:1, 2

*Original pronouns are singular.

CALLS TO WORSHIP

One thing have we* asked of the Lord,
   that will we seek after;
that we may dwell in the house of the Lord
   all the days of our lives,
to behold the beauty of the Lord,
and to inquire in his temple.

Ps. 27:4

Ascribe to the Lord, O heavenly beings,
   ascribe to the Lord glory and strength.
Ascribe to the Lord the glory of his name;
   worship the Lord in holy array.

Ps. 29:1, 2

I will bless the Lord at all times;
   his praise shall continually be in my mouth.
My soul makes its boast in the Lord;
   let the afflicted hear and be glad.
O magnify the Lord with me,
   and let us exalt his name together!

Ps. 34:1-3

*Original pronouns are singular.

O come, let us worship and bow down,
   let us kneel before the Lord, our Maker!
For he is our God,
   and we are the people of his pasture,
   and the sheep of his hand.

Ps. 95:6, 7

O sing to the Lord a new song;
   sing to the Lord, all the earth!
Sing to the Lord, bless his name;
   tell of his salvation from day to day.
Declare his glory among the nations,
   his marvelous works among all the peoples!
For great is the Lord, and greatly to be praised.

Ps. 96:1-4

Ascribe to the Lord, O families of the peoples,
   ascribe to the Lord glory and strength!
Ascribe to the Lord the glory due his name;
   bring an offering, and come into his courts!
Worship the Lord in holy array;
   tremble before him, all the earth!

Ps. 96:7-9

Praise the Lord!
O give thanks to the Lord,
   for he is good;
    for his steadfast love endures for ever!

Ps. 106:1-3

What shall *we render to the Lord
   for all his bounty to us?
We will lift up the cup of salvation
   and call on the name of the Lord,
We will pay our vows to the Lord
   in the presence of all his people.

Ps. 116:12-14

Praise the Lord, all nations!
Extol him, all peoples!
For great is his steadfast love toward us;
   and the faithfulness of the Lord
     endures for ever.
Praise the Lord!

Ps. 117

*Original pronouns are singular.

Make a joyful noise to the Lord, all the earth;
   break forth into joyous song and sing praises!
Sing praises to the Lord with the lyre,
   with the lyre and sound of melody!
With trumpets and the sound of the horn
   make a joyful noise before the King, the Lord!

Ps. 98:4-6

Make a joyful noise to the Lord, all the lands!
Serve the Lord with gladness!
Come into his presence with singing!
Know that the Lord is God!
It is he that made us, and we are his;
we are his people, and the sheep of his pasture.

Ps. 100:1-3

O give thanks to the Lord,
   call on his name,
   make known his deeds among the peoples!
Sing to him, sing praises to him,
   tell of all his wonderful works!

Ps. 105:1, 2

How lovely is thy dwelling place,
  O Lord of hosts!
My soul longs, yea, faints
  for the courts of the Lord;
my heart and flesh sing for joy to the living God.

Ps. 84:1-2

O come, let us sing to the Lord;
  let us make a joyful noise to the rock
    of our salvation!
Let us come into his presence with thanksgiving!
  let us make a joyful noise to him
    with songs of praise!
For the Lord is a great God,
  and a great King above all gods.

Ps. 95:1-3

Come, bless the Lord,
  all you servants of the Lord,
  who stand by night in the house of the Lord!
Lift up your hands to the holy place,
  and bless the Lord!

Ps. 134:1, 2

Appropriate for an evening service.

It is good to give thanks to the Lord,
   to sing praises to thy name,
     O Most High;
to declare thy steadfast love in the morning,
   and thy faithfulness by night.

Ps. 92:1-2

Appropriate for an outdoor service.

Bless the Lord, O my soul!
   O Lord my God, thou art very great!
Thou art clothed with honor and majesty,
   who coverest thyself with light
     as with a garment,
   who hast stretched out the heavens like a tent,
   who hast laid the beams of thy chambers
     on the waters,
   who makest the clouds thy chariot,
   who ridest on the wings of the wind,
   who makest the winds thy messengers,
     fire and flame thy ministers.
Bless the Lord, O my soul!
   Praise the Lord!

Ps. 104:1-4, 35b

Appropriate for a service by ocean or lake.

O Lord, how manifold are thy works!
In wisdom hast thou made them all;
   the earth is full of thy creatures.
Yonder is the sea, great and wide,
   which teems with things innumerable.
   living things both small and great.
May the glory of the Lord endure for ever,
   may the Lord rejoice in his works.

Ps. 104:24-25, 31

(Most of Psalm 104 is appropriate for out-of-doors worship.)

This is the day which the Lord has made;
   let us rejoice and be glad in it.

Ps. 118:24

Praise the Lord!
Sing to the Lord a new song,
   his praise in the assembly of the faithful!

Ps. 149:1

I was glad when they said to me,
"Let us go to the house of the Lord!"

Ps. 122:1

Praise the Lord!
Praise the Lord from the heavens,
    praise him in the heights!
Praise him, all his angels,
    praise him, all his host!
Praise him, sun and moon,
    praise him, all you shining stars!
Praise him, you highest heavens,
    and you waters above the heavens!
Praise the Lord!

Ps. 148:1-4, 14b

"The hour is coming, and now is,
when the true worshipers
will worship the Father in spirit and truth,
for such the Father seeks
to worship him."

John 4:23

Praise the Lord!
Praise God in his sanctuary;
 praise him in his mighty firmament!
Praise him for his mighty deeds;
 praise him according to his exceeding greatness!
Praise him with trumpet sound;
 praise him with lute and harp!
Praise him with timbrel and dance;
 praise him with strings and pipe!
Praise him with sounding cymbals;
 praise him with loud clashing cymbals!
Let everything that breathes praise the Lord!
Praise the Lord!

Ps. 150

Can be done antiphonally with Pastor and choir.

With what shall I come before the Lord,
 and bow myself before God on high?
He has showed you, O man, what is good;
 and what does the Lord require of you
 but to do justice,
 and to love kindness,
 and to walk humbly with your God?

Mic. 6:6a, 8

Praise the Lord!
For it is good to sing praises to our God;
   for he is gracious,
   and a song of praise is seemly.

Ps. 147:1

"This is none other than the house of God, and
this is the gate of heaven."

Gen. 28:17

Therefore, brethren, since we have confidence to enter the sanctuary by the blood of
Jesus . . . let us draw near with a true heart in
full assurance of faith, with our hearts sprinkled
clean from an evil conscience.

Heb. 10:19, 22

Let us consider how to stir up one another to
love and good works, not neglecting to meet
together, as is the habit of some, but encourag-
ing one another, and all the more as you see the
Day drawing near.

Heb. 10:24-25

"God is spirit, and those who worship him must
worship in spirit and truth."

John 4:24

Palm Sunday

Hosanna to the Son of David!
Blessed be he who comes in the name of the Lord!
Hosanna in the highest!

Matt. 21:9

Easter

O death, where is thy victory?
O death, where is thy sting?
But thanks be to God, who gives us the victory
through our Lord Jesus Christ.

I Cor. 15:55, 57

Easter Sunday Evening

On the evening of that day, the first day of the
week . . . Jesus came and stood among them
and said to them, "Peace be with you."

John 20:19

Advent

Lift up your heads, O gates!
　and be lifted up, O ancient doors!
　　that the King of glory may come in!
Who is this King of glory?
　The Lord of hosts,
　he is the King of glory!

Ps. 24:9, 10

Prepare the way of the Lord,
　make his paths straight.
Every valley shall be filled,
　and every mountain and hill shall be brought low,
　and the crooked shall be made straight,
　and the rough ways shall be made smooth;
and all flesh shall see the salvation of God.

Luke 3:4b-6

Advent and Christmas

And the Word became flesh and dwelt among us, full of grace and truth; we have beheld his glory, glory as of the only Son from the Father.

John 1:14

Let us go over to Bethlehem and see thing that has happened, which the Lord has made known to us.

Luke 2:15

Glory to God in the highest,
and on earth peace, good will toward men.

Luke 2:14, KJV

*Our souls magnify the Lord,
and our spirits rejoice in God our Savior.

Luke 1:46b-47

Blessed be the Lord God of Israel,
    for he has visited and redeemed his people,
and has raised up a horn of salvation for us
    in the house of his servant David,
as he spoke by the mouth of his holy prophets
    from of old.

Luke 1:68, 69

*Original pronouns are singular.

THE LAW OF GOD

THE LAW OF GOD

The Ten Commandments

And God spoke all these words, saying,

"I am the Lord your God, who brought you out of Egypt, out of the house of bondage.

"You shall have no other gods before me.

"You shall not make for yourself a graven image, or any likeness of anything that is in heaven above, or that is in the earth beneath, or that is in the water under the earth; you shall not bow down to them or serve them; for I the Lord your God am a jealous God, visiting the iniquity of the fathers upon the children to the third and the fourth generation of those who hate me, but showing steadfast love to thousands of those who love me and keep my commandments.

"You shall not take the name of the Lord your God in vain; for the Lord will not hold him guiltless who takes his name in vain.

"Remember the sabbath day, to keep it holy. Six days you shall labor, and do all your work; but the seventh day is a sabbath to the Lord your God; in it you shall not do any work, you, or your son, or your daughter, your manservant, or your maidservant, or your cattle, or the sojourner who is within your gates; for in six days the Lord made heaven and earth, the sea, and all that is in them, and rested the seventh day;

therefore the Lord blessed the sabbath day and hallowed it.

"Honor your father and your mother, that your days may be long in the land which the Lord your God gives you.

"You shall not kill.

"You shall not commit adultery.

"You shall not steal.

"You shall not bear false witness against your neighbor.

"You shall not covet your neighbor's house; you shall not covet your neighbor's wife, or his manservant, or his maidservant, or his ox, or his ass, or anything that is your neighbor's."

Exod. 20:1-17

Jesus' Summary of The Law

You shall love the Lord your God with all your heart, and with all your soul, and with all your mind. This is the great and first commandment. And a second is like it, You shall love your neighbor as yourself. On these two commandments depend all the law and the prophets.

Matt. 22:37-40

Summary of The Ten Commandments

You shall have no other gods before me.

You shall not make for yourself a graven image.

You shall not take the name of the Lord your god in vain.

Remember the sabbath day, to keep it holy.

Honor your father and your mother.

You shall not kill.

You shall not commit adultery.

You shall not steal.

You shall not bear false witness.

You shall not covet.

Exod. 20:1-17, selected

I appeal to you therefore, brethren, by the mercies of God, to present your bodies as a living sacrifice, holy and acceptable to God, which is your spiritual worship.

Do not be conformed to this world but be transformed by the renewal of your mind, that you may prove what is the will of God, what is good and acceptable and perfect.

Rom. 12:1, 2

Jesus' New Commandment

A new commandment I give to you, that you love one another; even as I have loved you.

John 13:34

What shall we say then? Are we to continue in sin that grace may abound? By no means! How can we who died to sin still live in it? Do you not know that all of us who have been baptized into Christ Jesus were baptized into his death? We were buried therefore with him by baptism into death, so that as Christ was raised from the dead by the glory of the Father, we too might walk in newness of life.

Rom. 6:14

I therefore, a prisoner for the Lord, beg you to lead a life worthy of the calling to which you have been called, with all lowliness and meekness, with patience, forbearing one another in love, eager to maintain the unity of the Spirit in the bond of peace.

Eph. 4:1-3

Hear, O Israel: The Lord our God is one Lord; and you shall love the Lord your God with all your heart, and with all your soul, and with all your might.

And these words which I command you this day shall be upon your heart; and you shall teach them diligently to your children, and shall talk of them when you sit in your house, and when you walk by the way, and when you lie down, and when you rise.

Deut. 6:4-7

He has showed you, O man, what is good;
    and what does the Lord require of you,
        but to do justice,
        and to love kindness,
        and to walk humbly with your God?
Mic. 6:8

Finally, brethren, whatever is true, whatever is honorable, whatever is just, whatever is pure, whatever is lovely, whatever is gracious, if there is any excellence, if there is anything worthy of praise, think about these things.

Phil. 4:8

Let love be genuine; hate what is evil, hold fast to what is good; love one another with brotherly affection; outdo one another in showing honor. Never flag in zeal, be aglow with the Spirit, serve the Lord. Rejoice in your hope, be patient in tribulation, be constant in prayer. Contribute to the needs of the saints, practice hospitality.

Bless those who persecute you; bless and do not curse them. Rejoice with those who rejoice, weep with those who weep. Live in harmony with one another; do not be haughty, but associate with the lowly; never be conceited. Repay no one evil for evil, but take thought for what is noble in the sight of all. If possible, so far as it depends upon you, live peaceably with all.

Rom. 12:9-18

Put off your old nature which belongs to your former manner of life and is corrupt through deceitful lusts, and be renewed in the spirit of your minds, and put on the new nature, created after the likeness of God in true righteousness and holiness.

Eph. 4:22-24

Let not sin therefore reign in your mortal bodies, to make you obey their passions. Do not yield your members to sin as instruments of wickedness, but yield yourselves to God as men who have been brought from death to life, and your members to God as instruments of righteousness. For sin will have no dominion over you, since you are not under law but under grace.

Rom. 6:12-14

Beloved, let us love one another; for love is of God, and he who loves is born of God and knows God. He who does not love does not know God; for God is love. In this the love of God was made manifest among us, that God sent his only Son into the world, so that we might live through him. In this is love, not that we loved God but that he loved us and sent his Son to be the expiation for our sins. Beloved, if God so loved us, we also ought to love one another. No man has ever seen God; if we love one another, God abides in us and his love is perfected in us.

I John 4:7-12

Put on then, as God's chosen ones, holy and beloved, compassion, kindness, lowliness, meekness, and patience, forbearing one another and, if one has a complaint against each other, forgiving each other; as the Lord has forgiven you, so you also must forgive.

And above all these put on love, which binds everything together in perfect harmony. And let the peace of Christ rule in your hearts, to which indeed you were called in the one body. And be thankful.

Col. 3:12-15

Therefore, since we are surrounded by so great a cloud of witnesses, let us also lay aside every weight, and sin which clings so closely, and let us run with perseverance the race that is set before us, looking to Jesus the pioneer and perfector of our faith, who for the joy that was set before him endured the cross, despising the shame, and is seated at the right hand of the throne of God.

Heb. 12:1, 2

OFFERTORY SENTENCES

Offer to God a sacrifice of thanksgiving,
and pay your vows to the Most High.
Ps. 50:14

Whatever you wish that men would do to you, do so to them; for this is the law and the prophets.

Matt. 7:12

Bring the full tithes into the storehouse, that there may be food in my house; and thereby put me to the test, says the Lord of hosts, if I will not open the windows of heaven for you and pour down for you an overflowing blessing.

Mal. 3:10

And he said to all, "If any man would come after me, let him deny himself and take up his cross daily and follow me."

Luke 9:23

Ascribe to the Lord the glory due his name;
  bring an offering, and come into his courts!

Ps. 96:8

Honor the Lord with your substance
  and with the first fruits of all your produce.

Prov. 3:9

And going into the house they saw the child
with Mary his mother, and they fell down and
worshiped him. Then, opening their treasures,
they offered him gifts, gold, frankincense and
myrrh.

Matt. 2:11

No servant can serve two masters; for either
he will hate the one and love the other, or he
will be devoted to the one and despise the other.
You cannot serve God and mammon.

Luke 16:13

If you are offering your gift at the altar, and there remember that your brother has something against you, leave your gift there before the altar and go; first be reconciled to your brother, and then come and offer your gift.

Matt. 5:23, 24

Beware of practicing your piety before men in order to be seen by them; for then you will have no reward from your Father who is in heaven. Thus, when you give alms, sound no trumpet before you, as the hypocrites do in the synagogues and in the streets, that they may be praised by men.

Matt. 6:1, 2

For in a severe test of affliction, their abundance of joy and their extreme poverty have overflowed in a wealth of liberality on their part. For they gave according to their means, as I can testify, and beyond their means, of their own free will.

II Cor. 8:2, 3

Truly, I say to you, as you did it to one of the least of these my brethren, you did it to me.

Matt. 25:40

Take heed, and beware of all covetousness; for a man's life does not consist in the abundance of his possessions.

Luke 12:15

And Zacchaeus stood and said to the Lord, "Behold, Lord, the half of my goods I give to the poor; and if I have defrauded any one of anything, I restore it fourfold."

Luke 19:8

Now as you excel in everything—in faith, in utterance, in knowledge, in all earnestness, and in your love for us—see that you excel in this gracious work also.

II Cor. 8:7

It is more blessed to give than to receive.

Acts 20:35

The point is this: he who sows sparingly will also reap sparingly, and he who sows bountifully will also reap bountifully.

II Cor. 9:6

Each one must do as he has made up his mind, not reluctantly or under compulsion, for God loves a cheerful giver.

II Cor. 9:7

You will be enriched in every way for great generosity, which through us will produce thanksgiving to God; for the rendering of his service not only supplies the wants of the saints but also overflows in many thanksgivings to God.

II Cor. 9:11, 12

God is able to provide you with every blessing in abundance, so that you may always have enough of everything and may provide in abundance for every good work.

II Cor. 9:8

PRAYERS OF CONFESSION

To thee, O Lord, *we lift up our souls.
Make us to know thy ways, O Lord;
    teach us thy paths.
Lead us in thy truth, and teach us,
    for thou art the God of our salvation;
    for thee we wait all the day long.
Be mindful of thy mercy, O Lord,
    and of thy steadfast love,
    for they have been from old.
Remember not the sins of our youth,
    or our transgressions;
    according to thy steadfast love remember us.
For thy name's sake, O Lord,
    pardon our guilt, for it is great.
Turn thou to us, and be gracious to us;
    for we are lonely and afflicted.
Relieve the troubles of our hearts,
    and bring us out of our distresses.
Consider our affliction and our trouble,
    and forgive all our sins.

Ps. 25:1, 4-7, 11, 16-18

*Original pronouns are singular.

Have mercy on *us, O God,
    according to thy steadfast love;
    according to thy abundant mercy
    blot out our transgressions.
Wash us thoroughly from our iniquities,
    and cleanse us from our sin!
For we know our transgressions,
    and our sin is ever before us.
Against thee, thee only have we sinned,
    and done that which is evil in thy sight,
so that thou art justified in thy sentence
    and blameless in thy judgment.
Purge us with hyssop, and we shall be clean;
    wash us, and we shall be whiter than snow.
Create in us clean hearts, O God,
    and put a new and right spirit within us.
Cast us not away from thy presence,
    and take not thy holy Spirit from us.
Restore to us the joy of thy salvation,
    and uphold us with a willing spirit.
The sacrifice acceptable to God is a broken spirit;
    a broken and contrite heart, O God,
    thou wilt not despise.

Ps. 51:1-4, 7, 10-12, 17

*Original pronouns are singular.

Do not thou, O Lord,
    withhold thy mercy from *us,
  let thy steadfast love and thy faithfulness
    ever preserve us!
For evils have encompassed us without number;
    our iniquities have overtaken us,
    till we cannot see;
  they are more than the hairs of our heads;
    our hearts fail us.
Be pleased, O Lord, to deliver us!
  O Lord, make haste to help us!

Ps. 40:11-13

To thee *we lift up our eyes,
O thou who art enthroned in the heavens!
Behold, as the eyes of servants
  look to the hand of their master,
as the eyes of a maid
  to the hand of her mistress,
so our eyes look to the Lord our God,
  till he have mercy upon us.
Have mercy upon us, O Lord,
  have mercy upon us.

Ps. 123:1-3a

*Original pronouns are singular.

O Lord, rebuke *us not in thy anger,
    nor chasten us in thy wrath!
For thy arrows have sunk into us,
    and thy hand has come down on us.
There is no soundness in our flesh
    because of thy indignation;
  there is no health in our bones
    because of our sin.
For our iniquities have gone over our heads;
    they weigh like a burden too heavy for us.
We confess our iniquities,
    we are sorry for our sins.
Do not forsake us, O Lord!
    O our God, be not far from us!
Make haste to help us,
    O Lord, our salvation!

Ps. 38:1-4, 18, 21-22

*Original pronouns are singular.

Out of the depths we cry to thee,
   O Lord!
Lord, hear our voices!
Let thy ears be attentive
   to the voice of our supplications!
If thou, O Lord, shouldst mark iniquities,
   Lord, who could stand?
But there is forgiveness with thee,
   that thou mayest be feared.

Ps. 130:1-4

*(Suggestion: Use Psalm 130:7, 8 for Assurance
   of Pardon.)*

ASSURANCES OF PARDON

Blessed is he whose transgression is forgiven,
  whose sin is covered.
Blessed is the man to whom the Lord
  imputes no iniquity,
and in whose spirit there is no deceit.

Ps. 21:1, 2

Bless the Lord, O my soul;
  and all that is within me
  bless his holy name!
Bless the Lord, O my soul,
  and forget not all his benefits,
who forgives all your iniquity,
  who heals all your diseases,
who redeems your life from the Pit,
  who crowns you with steadfast love and mercy,
who satisfies you with good as long as you live
  so that your youth is renewed like the eagle's.

Ps. 103:1-5

I tell you, there is joy before the angels of God
over one sinner who repents.

Luke 15:10

The Lord is merciful and gracious,
   slow to anger and abounding in steadfast love.
He does not deal with us according to our sins,
   nor requite us according to our iniquities.
For as the heavens are high above the earth,
   so great is his steadfast love
   toward those who fear him;
as far as the east is from the west,
   so far does he remove our transgressions from us.

Ps. 103:8, 10-12

[Jesus said,] Come unto me, all who labor and are heavy-laden, and I will give you rest. Take my yoke upon you and learn from me, for I am gentle and lowly in heart, and you will find rest for your souls.

Matt. 11:28, 29

As Moses lifted up the serpent in the wilderness, so must the Son of Man be lifted up, that whoever believes in him may have eternal life.

John 3:14, 15

O Israel, hope in the Lord!
 For with the Lord there is steadfast love,
 and with him is plenteous redemption.
And he will redeem Israel
 from all his iniquities.

Ps. 130:7, 8

(Suggestion: use in conjunction with Prayer of Confession, Psalm 130:1-4)

Jesus . . . said . . . Truly, truly, I say to you, I am the door of the sheep. All who come before me are thieves and robbers; but the sheep did not heed them. I am the door; if any one enters by me, he will be saved.

John 10:7-9

[Jesus said] My sheep hear my voice, and I know them, and they follow me; and I give them eternal life, and they shall never perish, and no one shall snatch them out of my hand. I and the Father are one.

John 10:27-28, 30

For God so loved the world that he gave his only Son, that whoever believes in him should not perish but have eternal life.

John 3:16

For God sent the Son into the world, not to condemn the world, but that the world might be saved through him.

John 3:17

Repent therefore, and turn again, that your sins may be blotted out, that times of refreshing may come from the presence of the Lord.

Acts 3:19

Likewise the Spirit helps us in our weakness; for we do not know how to pray as we ought, but the Spirit himself intercedes for us with sighs too deep for words.

Rom. 8:26

And there is salvation in no one else, for there is no other name under heaven given among men by which we must be saved.

Acts 4:12

Therefore, since we are justified by faith, we have peace with God through our Lord Jesus Christ.

Rom. 5:1

Wretched man that I am! Who will deliver me from this body of death? Thanks be to God through Jesus Christ our Lord!

Rom. 7:24, 25a

The Lord is not slow about his promise as some count slowness, but is forbearing toward you, not wishing that any should perish, but that all should reach repentance.

II Peter 3:9

God shows his love for us in that while we were yet sinners Christ died for us.

Rom. 5:8

If God is for us, who is against us?
He who did not spare his own Son
but gave him up for us all,
will he not also give us all things with him?
Who shall bring any charge against God's elect?
It is God who justifies; who is to condemn?

Rom. 8:31-34a

For I am sure that
   neither death, nor life,
   nor angels, nor principalities,
   nor things present, nor things to come,
   nor powers,
   nor height, nor depth,
   nor anything else in all creation,
will be able to separate us from the love of God
in Christ Jesus our Lord.

Rom. 8:38, 39

For you did not receive the spirit of slavery to fall back into fear, but you have received the spirit of sonship. When we cry, "Abba! Father!" it is the Spirit himself bearing witness with our spirit that we are children of God, and if children, then heirs, heirs of God and fellow heirs with Christ.

Rom. 8:15-17a

For I know whom I have believed, and am persuaded that he is able to keep that which I have committed unto him against that day.

II Tim. 1:12 (KJV)

He saved us, not because of deeds done by us in righteousness, but in virtue of his own mercy, by the washing of regeneration and renewal in the Holy Spirit, which he poured out upon us richly through Jesus Christ our Lord, so that we might be justified by his grace and become heirs in hope of eternal life.

Titus 3:5-7

There is therefore now no condemnation for those who are in Christ Jesus.

Rom. 8:1

My little children, I am writing this to you so that you may not sin; but if any one does sin, we have an advocate with the Father, Jesus Christ the righteous; and he is the expiation for our sins, and not for ours only but also for the sins of the whole world.

I John 2:1, 2

He himself bore our sins in his body on the tree, that we might die to sin and live to righteousness. By his wounds you have been healed.

I Peter 2:24

I write this to you who believe in the name of the Son of God, that you may know that you have eternal life.

I John 5:13

For we have not a high priest who is unable to sympathize with our weaknesses, but one who in every respect has been tempted as we are, yet without sinning. Let us then with confidence draw near to the throne of grace, that we may receive mercy and find grace to help in time of need.

Heb. 4:15, 16

Those whom I love, I reprove and chasten;
   so be zealous and repent.
Behold, I stand at the door and knock;
if any one hears my voice and opens the door,
   I will come in to him and eat with him,
      and he with me.

Rev. 3:19, 20

If we say we have no sin, we deceive ourselves, and the truth is not in us. If we confess our sins, he is faithful and just, and will forgive our sins and cleanse us from all unrighteousness.

I John 1:8, 9

READINGS FOR COMMUNION

Who has believed what we have heard?
And to whom has the arm of the Lord
    been revealed?
For he grew up before him like a young plant,
    and like a root out of dry ground;
he had no form or comeliness
    that we should look at him,
    and no beauty that we should desire him.
He was despised and rejected by men;
    a man of sorrows, and acquainted with grief;
and as one from whom men hide their faces
    he was despised, and we esteemed him not.
Surely he has borne our griefs
    and carried our sorrows;
yet we esteemed him stricken,
    smitten by God, and afflicted.
But he was wounded for our transgressions,
    he was bruised for our iniquities;
upon him was the chastisement that made us whole,
    and with his stripes we are healed.
All we like sheep have gone astray;
    we have turned every one to his own way;
and the Lord has laid on him
    the iniquity of us all.

Isa. 53:1-6

Behold, the days are coming, says the Lord, when I will make a new covenant with the house of Israel and the house of Judah, not like the covenant which I made with their fathers when I took them by the hand to bring them out of the land of Egypt, my covenant which they broke, though I was their husband, says the Lord. But this is the covenant which I will make with the house of Israel after those days, says the Lord: I will put my law within them, and I will write it upon their hearts; and I will be their God, and they shall be my people.

Jer. 31:31-33

Now as they were eating, Jesus took bread, and blessed, and broke it, and gave it to the disciples and said, "Take, eat; this is my body." And he took a cup, and when he had given thanks he gave it to them, saying, "Drink of it, all of you; for this is my blood of the covenant, which is poured out for many for the forgiveness of sins. I tell you I shall not drink again of this fruit of the vine until that day when I drink it new with you in my Father's kingdom."

Matt. 26:26-29

Jesus then took the loaves, and when he had given thanks, he distributed them to those who were seated; so also the fish, as much as they wanted. And when they had eaten their fill, he told his disciples, "Gather up the fragments left over, that nothing may be lost." So they gathered them up and filled twelve baskets with fragments from the five barley loaves, left by those who had eaten. When the people saw the sign which he had done, they said, "This is indeed the prophet who is to come into the world!"

John 6:11-14

For I received from the Lord what I also delivered to you, that the Lord Jesus on the night when he was betrayed took bread, and when he had given thanks, he broke it, and said, "This is my body which is for you. Do this in remembrance of me." In the same way also the cup, after supper, saying, "This cup is the new covenant in my blood. Do this, as often as you drink it, in remembrance of me." For as often as you eat this bread and drink the cup, you proclaim the Lord's death until he comes.

I Cor. 11:23-26

[Jesus said,] "I am the bread of life. Your fathers ate the manna in the wilderness, and they died. This is the bread which comes down from heaven, that a man may eat of it and not die. I am the living bread which came down from heaven; if any one eats of this bread, he will live for ever; and the bread which I shall give for the life of the world is my flesh."

John 6:48-51

The cup of blessing which we bless, is it not a participation in the blood of Christ? The bread which we break, is it not a participation in the body of Christ? Because there is one loaf, we who are many are one body, for we all partake of the same loaf.

I Cor. 10:16, 17

Examine yourselves, to see whether you are holding to your faith. Test yourselves. Do you not realize that Jesus Christ is in you?—unless indeed you fail to meet the test!

II Cor. 13:5

Whoever, therefore, eats the bread or drinks the cup of the Lord in an unworthy manner will be guilty of profaning the body and blood of the Lord. Let a man examine himself, and so eat of the bread and drink of the cup. For any one who eats and drinks without discerning the body eats and drinks judgment upon himself.

I Cor. 11:27-29

BENEDICTIONS

The Lord bless you and keep you:
The Lord make his face to shine upon you,
    and be gracious to you:
The Lord lift up his countenance upon you,
    and give you peace.

Num. 6:24-26

Surely goodness and mercy shall follow *us
    all the days of our lives,
and we shall dwell in the house of the Lord for ever.

Ps. 23:6

The Lord is your keeper;
    the Lord is your shade on your right hand.
The sun shall not smite you by day,
    nor the moon by night.
The Lord will keep you from all evil;
    he will keep your life.
The Lord will keep your going out
    and your coming in
      from this time forth and for evermore.

Ps. 121:5-8

*Original pronouns are singular.

Suitable for Christmas

Lord, now lettest thou thy servants* depart in peace,
   according to thy word;
for our eyes have seen thy salvation
  which thou hast prepared in the presence
    of all peoples,
  a light for revelation to the Gentiles,
  and for glory to thy people Israel.

Luke 2:29-32

Go therefore and make disciples of all nations,
baptizing them in the name of the Father and of
the Son and of the Holy Spirit, teaching them to
observe all that I have commanded you; and lo,
I am with you always, to the close of the age.

Matt. 28:19, 20

The grace of the Lord Jesus Christ and the
love of God and the fellowship of the Holy Spirit
be with you all.

II Cor. 13:14

*Original pronouns are singular.

Agree with one another, live in peace, and the God of love and peace will be with you.

II Cor. 13:11b

Now to him who by the power at work within us is able to do far more abundantly than all that we ask or think, to him be glory in the church and in Christ Jesus to all generations, for ever and ever. Amen.

Eph. 3:20, 21

Peace be to the brethren, and love with faith, from God the Father, and the Lord Jesus Christ. Grace be with all who love our Lord Jesus Christ with love undying.

Eph. 6:23

The peace of God, which passes all understanding, will keep your hearts and your minds in Christ Jesus.

Phil. 4:7

Lead a life worthy of the calling to which you have been called, with all lowliness and meekness, with patience, forbearing one another in love, eager to maintain the unity of the Spirit in the bond of peace.

Eph. 4:1-3

Therefore, my beloved . . . work out your own salvation with fear and trembling; for God is at work in you, both to will and to work for his good pleasure.

Phil. 2:12, 13

God will supply every need of yours according to his riches in glory in Christ Jesus. To our God and Father be glory for ever and ever.

Phil. 4:19, 20

The grace of the Lord Jesus Christ be with your spirit.

Philem. 25

Let all bitterness and wrath and anger and clamor and slander be put away from you, with all malice, and be kind to one another, tenderhearted, forgiving one another, as God in Christ forgave you.

Eph. 4:31, 32

Finally, brethren, whatever is true, whatever is honorable, whatever is just, whatever is pure, whatever is lovely, whatever is gracious, if there is any excellence, if there is anything worthy of praise, think about these things.

Phil. 4:8

Now may the God of peace who brought again from the dead our Lord Jesus, the great shepherd of the sheep, by the blood of the eternal covenant, equip you with everything good that you may do his will, working in you that which is pleasing in his sight, through Jesus Christ; to whom be glory for ever and ever. Amen.

Heb. 13:20, 21

Now may our Lord Jesus Christ himself, and God our Father, who loved us and gave us eternal comfort and good hope through grace, comfort your hearts and establish them in every good work and word.

II Thess. 2:16, 17

Beware lest you be carried away with the error of lawless men and lose your own stability. But grow in the grace and knowledge of our Lord and Savior Jesus Christ. To him be the glory both now and to the day of eternity. Amen.

II Peter 3:17, 18

Now to him who is able to keep you from falling and to present you without blemish before the presence of his glory with rejoicing, to the only God, our Savior through Jesus Christ our Lord, be glory, majesty, dominion, and authority, before all time and now and for ever. Amen.

Jude 24, 25

May the God of peace himself sanctify you wholly; and may your spirit and soul and body be kept sound and blameless at the coming of our Lord Jesus Christ.

I Thess. 5:23

To the King of ages, immortal, invisible, the only God, be honor and glory for ever and ever. Amen.

I Tim. 1:17

Humble yourselves therefore under the mighty hand of God, that in due time he may exalt you. Cast all your anxieties on him, for he cares about you.

I Peter 5:6, 7